Contents

List of Figures

To my family

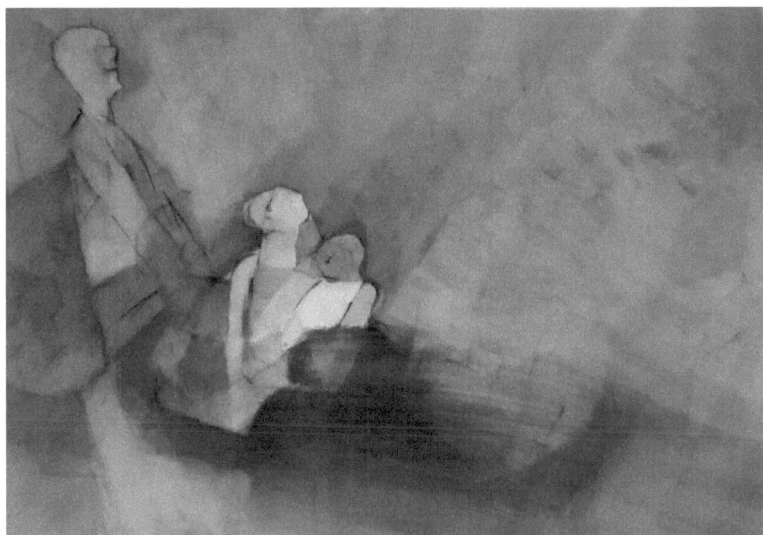

Foreword

Words wrapped around thought and feelings, caressing experience. I am delighted to share them with you and hope you will enjoy them as much as I enjoyed writing them. I am even more delighted that these words are coupled with the artwork of one of my favorite artists, Wolfgang Hirsch. Yes, we are related and I want to express my deep gratitude to Wolfgang that he made this collaboration possible before he passed in February of 2011.

I also want to thank my son Julian for his tireless efforts in teaching me the world of self publishing. Without you this book might have not come into existence. A collaboration that spans and connects three generations.

With great delight and gratitude

Katharina

Let the Heart Be Still

Let the heart be still, my love
The moment will explain.
The rain, the wind, the sun will show us the way
As our bodies will dance in the moonlight.
Tender words, reaching,
Meeting their target deeply,
Unable to speak directly
Not wanting the mind to take charge.
Shadows, some doubts still dancing
Reluctance to trust the change.
Be still, my love
And drink in the warmth of the moment.

Kiss of Remembrance

In the full moon night
I have been kissed into remembrance
And my body softens, melting into the caress.
Seeing the constant vigilance
That every cell has become accustomed to so clearly.
Dark shadows play against the bright of the light
A longing of fulfilment wants to make itself present
And falls short,
Drops into the void,
The remembrance stands, cells expanding fully
Into juicy warmth energized by the flow.
Oh, how can I forget this delicious dream!
But not today.
Today I have been kissed into remembrance.

It Cannot Be

I see you
And my heart jumps with joy.
I stand next to you
And there is no where else I want to be.
I experience something that touches me
And all I want to do is to tell you about it.
I do not need to know anything more
And you tell me
"This Love Can Not Be"

The Mind, a Perspective

The mind, perceived like the dentist.
No one likes it, seems bothersome, no painful.
What about its perspective?
"I am just doing what I am supposed to do.
I am designed to do mind stuff, made for it,
My speciality.
Thinking, computing, figuring things out,
I think I am very good at it.
How would you like it if you were always attacked?
Someone always trying to silence you, pacifying you,
A big yuck!
I am not the enemy. How could I be?"

Sitting here watching the birds on the water
An enormous compassion and kindness arises for the mind,
The gratefulness for a job well done.
In the moment acknowledged, not identified with,
It calms and takes its place
In the deliciousness of the silent dance.
Just one aspect of the wonder
Like one bird within the flock, dancing on the water.

Every word coming out of my mouth,
The mind masterfully justifying itself.
Brilliance! Hats off.
Aiming to escape the whirling, tumbling sense of
Overwhelm that threatens the very fiber of the fabric.
Feeling so very week, so tender,
Tears always ready for the taking.
Another mirage, seeming never-ending,
Tumbling, intertwined over and over into......
Yes.........- into what?
Downright comical
The absurdity of it all.
The spectrum from bliss to despair,
All the same.........what a joke.
And still trying to engage at all cost.
The sense of separateness lingering, hanging on,
And within all of it gratefulness arises.

Moon Maiden

The moon maiden.
Her world the deep, the unconscious,
Filled with shadows, dancing in the silver light.

I see her walking on the moonbeam
Across the water with light steps
Crossing the body of the senses.
Her soft, rich womb welcoming all fears,
Easily transcended in the light.

The moon maiden, laughing like a bubbling brook
As she plays in the world of shadows.
Covered by the blanket of the night.
Crystal bells accompanying her song,
Eerie caressing the silvery beam of the moon.

Moon maiden, your empire the world of dreams,
In splendor.
Your essence present in every pore of my being
As I drink your sweet nectar that flows in the light.

Dance With Me

My Doctorate, My PHD,
Not about you, all about me.
I found the perfect mirage,
The one that incorporates it all,
All hopes and wishes and all nightmares to boot.
The best of all worlds and the worst to be sure.
Yes to your withdrawal!
Yes to your secrecy!
Yes to your turning hot and cold on a dime!
Irrational, not understandable,
Not a clue of who you are.
I imagine you like it that way
As I hear your scream to be seen.
I will fight no more.
Not with me, not with you and not with the world.
I lay down my judgement, my attack, my defence, my
readiness to pounce, my sword.
The world is too full of magic and wonder to want to
engage in war.
Dance with me, dance with me, dance with me,
My call to you,
No answer. . .

But my heart calls nevertheless.
Nothing for me to do.
I imagine the dragon will want to show her roar again
At different times.
I will wrap her in kindness,
Cradle her and offer her "play with your fire instead."
Maybe a weenie roast?
Curiosity prevails.

Infinite Creativity

Let the child come out to play
And kiss the day into exsistance.
Let the streets be filled
With your laughter and your tears,
Then tie your red shoes and dance,
Lightly following the song that moves your heart.
Marvel at the wonder created every day
In every rock, leaf or plant.
Infinite ceativity
Displayed and lived in every breath.
The air will carry you- All is well.
Nothing to fear
Doubt so still
Breathe-
Receive-
Embrace-

Show Me Your Tears

Love me tomorrow
Love me today
Take me into your heart.
Caress me with smiles
And eyes that shine,
Bathe me in all your charms.
Tell me your sorrows
Show me your tears
Let uncertainty shine,
And when I breathe the last breath this time
I thank thee with all that I am.

The Dream

The magic dream,
Discernment clouded by a promise.
I thought of roses that bloom in ice and snow
No matter what season, the pedals unfold.
A dream, so old, embedded in man,
A song that is sung over and over again.
What holds my heart now is the moon in the night,
The sun with his warmth
The wind with its might.
The element of surprise, disillusionments twin
As I step lightly into the wind.

Thoughts on Peace

I am not against war
I embrace peace.
I am not against hate
I nurture compassion.
I am not against fighting
I learn understanding.
I am not against lies
I search for truth.
I heard you say "We must fight for Peace"
So I am asking you "How will we bring Peace into this
world when we rage war against ourselves?"
Deep down inside, the darkest fears and nightmares,
Wounds, perceived inadequacies and judgments,
Shunned, not seen, not wanted,
Growing steadily in tight cages,
Becoming monsters that walk the streets
Killing children, raping women, torturing men
And with greedy eyes looking for more, more and more.

A proposal, a new idea perhaps.
Let's invite them for tea.
"One lump or two?" you might offer.

Trying "Yes" instead of "No"
And then, as you are sitting with each other,
Eye to eye, seeing the other clearly,
Uncovering monsters as imposters,
Judgment can melt into the absence of belief.
In the absence of belief love shines,
Towing peace and compassion in its wake,
A side effect, to be sure.
So no need to fight, beloved.
I have never met a man with a peaceful heart
That rapes women, kills children or tortures beings.
So "Yes" is my answer.
Embrace

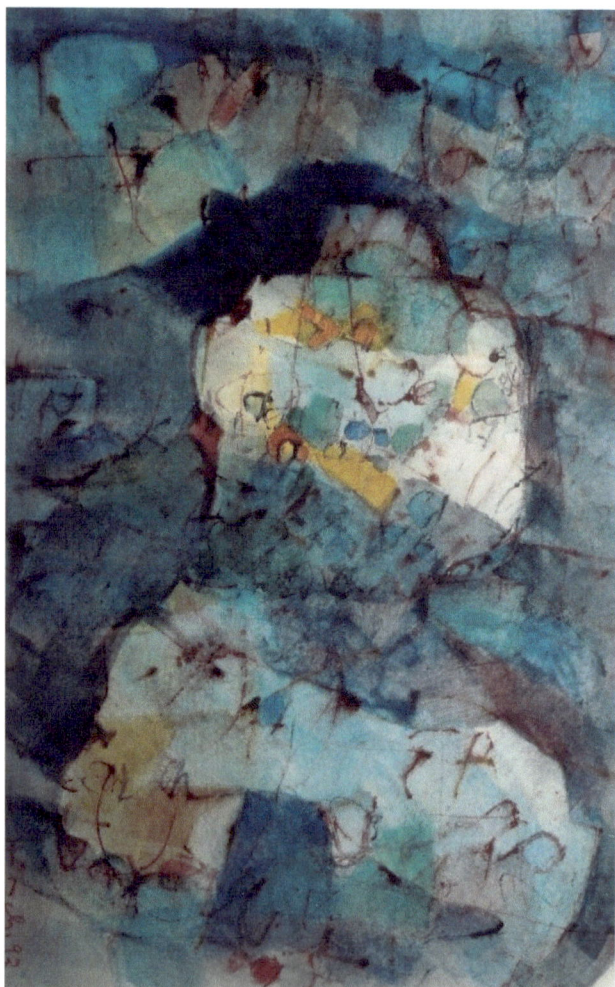

Talk to Me

Talk to me slowly
Talk to me straight
I want to hear what you got on your plate.
I want to taste your potatoes, your chicken,
Your ice cream,
So I know what it feels like to live in your dream.
Don't care if it's raw or present on a platter,
Just let me peak into that endless chatter.
We can laugh, shout or cry together,
Or simply be still in that moment forever...
A food fight you say?
That sounds ok.
Let's have the stuff fly, so we can stay
And enjoy the world in a different way.

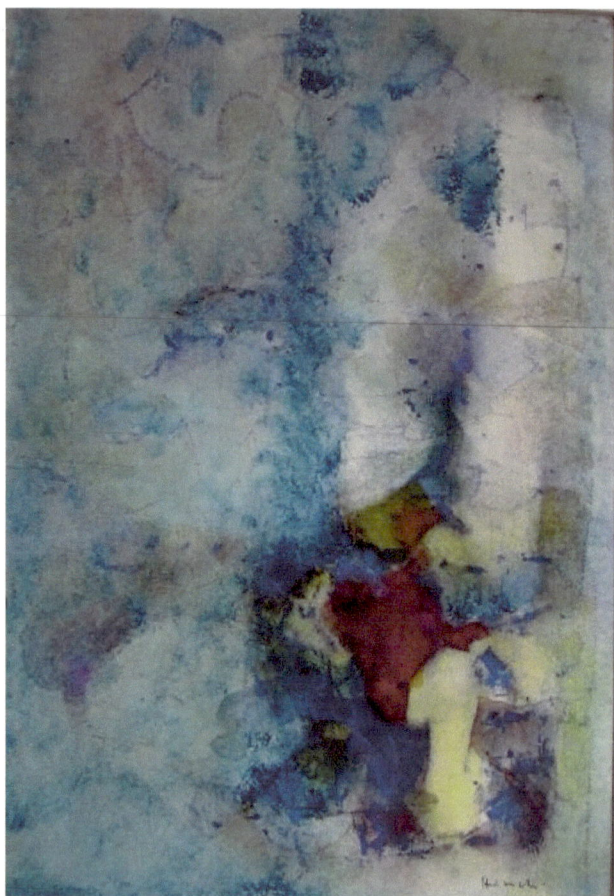

Sitting

The rich weave of the moment,
One thought,
The moment shed quickly by the focus of the eye.
Sitting in silence, discovering an ever tumbling depth,
Amazed at the rich fabric,
Lifetimes upon lifetimes, stretching, circling, never-ending.

The deliciousness, the agony, the silence.
"How can it be that all of this happens at once?"
The mind scrambles.
Smiles, peace, grace. . . the answer.
Really nothing to say-
But then again. . . . .

Owl and Crow

Tangled wings in the night
Fighting for the right of life.
Caught in headlights bright as day
Protective shadows whisked away.
Torn between flight and prey
Will she flee or will she stay?

Suddenly all rules have changed.
New hope for the one that has been slain.
Human presence brakes nature's flow of life and death,
Until at last the dies are cast.
The predator withdraws without the prey
Hoping to claim it another day.

I Sing and I Shout

An ocean of judgment, what do you see?
The world your mirror, me on my knees.
Shaking and trembling, head is exploding,
My heart is racing, eyes that are bulging.
The cords are elusive, the strings are off tone
As I sing my song with self-doubt in my bone.
This silliness screams to high heaven, no doubt.
What do I do?
I sing and I shout.
Sing my song over and over and over again,
That's all I do,
One moment, another and another my friend.
Sitting and noticing all that I feel,
The perception elusive the sensations seem real.
That's all that I know, that's all I can do.
I imagine it would do wonders for you too.
Let's try it together and stop being scared
Of you and me and what either might say.
Let judgment be judgment and delight be delight,
Accept everything in between as alright,
And with that my friend,
I am saying "Good night."

Vibration

Insecurity, expression, joy, magical sound within.
Finding the connection in vibration, your tone,
Your unique sound, so powerful, so clear.
Tears arise.
Nothing to say.
Recognition? Being seen?
Seeing oneself without noticing.
The sound occurs, springing with force and clarity.
Why is that so frightening?
The sinking into the unknown.
Uncontrollable.
The world seeing what is waiting,
Myself,
Feeling what is there.
Inside behind the veil so pure so tender,
So fragile with endless strength.
Just acceptance.
Seeing fears for fears, laughter for laughter,
Silence for silence.
No rewards, no illusions.
Terror for terror.

The walls are breaking, crumbling dry and old,
Making room for the new tender growth of spring.
What are we afraid of?
The boogeyman? Fear itself?
Crippling withdrawal and lies, hiding in our corner,
Gollum afraid to see the light.
What if we "loose ourselves"?
Isn't that what we desire by "falling in love"?
But then again so afraid to feel the moment.
Intimacy!
Understanding through the heart.
Ka—boom, ka—boom, beating, harmonizing, steady.
Still the greatest power on earth.
So be it.
May the towers fall, crumbling to the ground
While the trumpets announcing
Splendor of delight in expression.
Intimacy with Self,
Home residing in vibration.

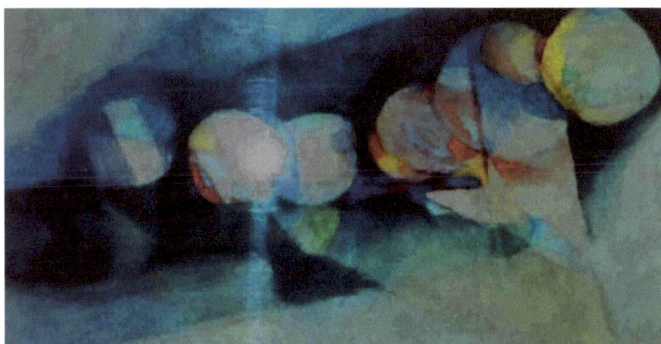

A Letter to My Right

Those mighty soldiers standing guard
Firmly rooted in contraction.
Holding the fortress for soo long,
Years of protection, years of fear.
Faces of scarred rigidity.
Once perceived, once called forth,
Once desperately built to defend.
Didn't anyone tell them that they are defending
Empty ground?!
What once seemed real no longer exists.
The habit of holding firm no longer needed.
"Dear guards, strip down your armor.
Let your skin be seen, it is time to breathe once again.
Lay down your weapons for they are not needed anymore.
Join hands so we can dance in balance once again.
Remember the times of early child's play,
Teeter—tottering in soothing flexibility and softness.
I know deep down you can,
Remember, remember, remember.........."
It's all that is needed.
And so be it
- Amen-

One Never Knows

I found myself walking down the road
Wondering what was disturbing me so.
Thinking, thinking, twisting and turning
Like a butter maker my insides
Were tumbling and churning.
I was cooking and stewing
As suddenly some light was quietly protruding,
Shifting the whole picture in its foundation.
Imagine my surprise. . .
When I looked I saw nothing,
Not even a reason for salvation.

Flowers

Flowers!
They celebrate the news
That our baby, now in shoes,
Walks, runs, and soon will skip;
Even though an occasional trip
Will make him cry.
Try nick, try, try
And soon you will fly.

Vashon

I am grateful for the wind and the rain on my skin,
The sheltering stars for me and my kin.
You cradled us softly and warm in your arms,
Your trees with strength, your sun with warmth.
The children grew strong and kind on this ground,
Explored their world in your rocks, sand and found-
A place where seeds grow roots that are deep and strong,
That nurture life for seasons to come.
I pray thee thanks for the life that I had
Here in this place that I called my pad.
My home, the very first one that I have ever known.
The words fail me for what I've been shown.
Here, on this island, in dreamtime I have grown
From mud to lotus.........
And now this life seems to come to an end,
Not my will, but this willow will bend.
The time has come to leave the nest
And explore new worlds, uncharted lands,
Old paths laid to rest.
I pray for life's richness to rest deep in my chest-
Where the rain and the wind touches my skin
In peace and communion with the rest of my kin.

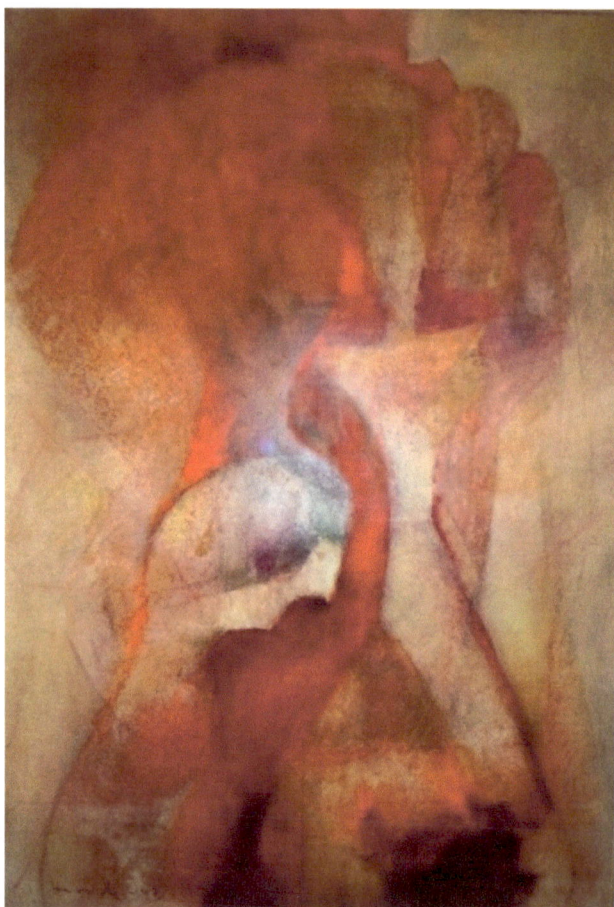

Kindle a Light

Don't be angry at the dark. Kindle a light!
Frustration, a thought born in pain,
Like the wind blowing through the valley
It will come and disperse again.
Don't be angry at the dark. Kindle a light!
Fairness has nothing to do with it,
A concept born through the beliefs of men.
Don't be angry at the dark. Kindle a light!
The illusion of personal love that comes and goes,
Disappointments born in expectations.
Don't be angry at the dark. Kindle a light!
Seperation,
Monster of aloneness waiting in the dark,
Threatening to devour all.........
And still,
Don't be angry at the dark. Kindle a light!
One trick Pony,
In kindness
With kindness
Through kindness

Jewels

I found a jewel on my path.
I stopped, looked and liked what I saw.
The impulse to seize it,
The wisdom to leave it.
Just the memory in my heart.

Love

It has all been said;
There is nothing to do.
Drink
Eat
Sleep
Sit
Love

The Authors

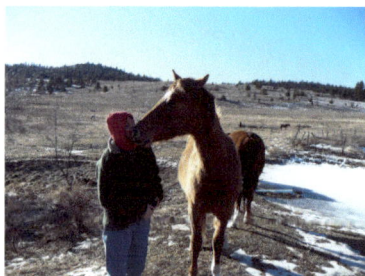

Katharina Hirsch

Katharina Hirsch was born in Berlin and moved to the US in 1976. Through poetry, dance, sculpting, singing and building she loves to play in expression. Katharina serves the moment as wisdom keeper, teacher and artist. In the past she has worked as primal therapist, make-up artist for stage and film, ceramic artist, energy worker and has led seminars for Qi Gong and BodyTalk.
She currently lives in Montana's Flathead Valley creating a permaculture garden and sanctuary to nurture life.
Please visit the websites:
www.khirsch.com
www.placeofgathering.com
www.w-hirsch.com

Wolfgang Hirsch
03.07.1924-02.02.2011
with grandson Julian Smith

For Wolfgang Hirsch painting, over and over again, was the exciting adventure to create an empty surface out of nothing by means of color and shape as well as experiences and inventions that he had made. "My painting is a bit like Bleigiessen" (german New Year's custom). What seems to be scribbling at first crystallizes into shapes, which may be mysterious and incomprehensible for the viewer, but for the painter they are very real. It may be compared to a child, who has the ability to breathe life into some building blocks, constructing the most curious things. The choice of color played an important role for Wolfgang Hirsch who predominantly used watercolor and gouache techniques. The artist's expression by means of color and allocation, provokes corresponding emotions within the viewer. His paintings should be comprehensible for the viewer, as crazy as they might be. The title, the name given to the painting, fulfills the function as key, giving the viewer access to the painting.

www.ingramcontent.com/pod-product-compliance
Lightning Source LLC
Chambersburg PA
CBHW041530090426

42738CB00035B/25